The
YULE LOG

RP Minis™
Hachette Book Group
1290 Avenue of the Americas, New York, NY 10104
www.runningpress.com
@Running_Press

First Edition: October 2020

Published by RP Minis, an imprint of Perseus Books, LLC, a subsidiary of Hachette Book Group, Inc. The RP Minis name and logo is a trademark of the Hachette Book Group.

The publisher is not responsible for websites (or their content) that are not owned by the publisher.

ISBN: 978-0-7624-7149-2

CONTENTS

Introduction

The holiday season is full of fun cold-weather traditions that leave you feeling holly, jolly, and ready for Christmas—picking out a picture-perfect Christmas tree, sledding down your favorite hill, or building the perfect snowman. Some traditions, though, don't really make you feel warm, fuzzy, and festive, like shoveling out the driveway, clearing ice off your car, and the daily trek to work in the slush. After those less-than-thrilling aspects of the season, it's important to thaw out to ward off the chill. So why don't you head back to your stately abode to curl up in front of a roaring hearth, tended to by your loyal servant?

What's that? You actually just got to your cubicle and someone stole your space heater last winter?

Well, lucky for you, you're holding in your hand the world's smallest Yule Log, inspired by one of the world's oldest Christmas traditions. This desktop or tabletop version is sure to leave you cozy and comfortable—without violating any fire codes! Bask in its soft glow and enjoy its gentle crackling while you read this book and learn about the ancient origins of the mysterious log and its modern journey to becoming a delicious dessert, a hit 1960s television program, and now a mainstay on screens everywhere during holiday parties.

P.S. Doris stole your space heater.

A *Log* and Storied History

So, how'd this log get so famous? Yule never guess.

To trace the history of the Yule Log, we have to go way back—back to at least the 1100s. Around that time, Celtic people—who believed that the sun stood still during the winter solstice, starting on December 21—got the idea that keeping a single log burning during the solstice would help encourage the sun to move again (and to, you know, brighten up and warm their chilly abodes). The log in question had to be carefully selected so that it would burn for twelve full days—so, really, we're talking

more about an entire tree than the logs you might throw into your fireplace today. Keeping that log burning, it was thought, would not only give the sun a nudge to come back out, but also ward off a host of evils and misfortunes. (Good

thing that today, YouTube allows us to "burn" a Yule Log nearly endlessly—no evil spirits here!)

As paganism evolved into Christianity (and maybe as people decided they didn't want to keep lugging gigantic tree trunks from the forest to their hearths), Yule Log traditions have continued, but on a much smaller scale. For centuries now, many families across the world have burned a log on Christmas Eve or Christmas Day to pay homage to the pagan tradition. While the practice has morphed many times over, with different religions, regions, and countries putting their own unique spin on the ceremony and tradition, the basic concept has remained the same: burning the Yule Log will bring good luck and good spirit to any Yuletide celebration.

Uh, What Does "Yule" Actually Mean?

The word "Yule" is what the Celts called the winter solstice and the name that Germanic pagans gave their midwinter festival lasting from mid-November to early January. Today, the term is basically congruous with "Christmastime" or "the period during which every store in America is plastered in red and green and tinsel." *Troll the ancient yuletide carol*, and all that!

The Modern Yule

Although most people aren't still chopping down oak trees and burning them for twelve days straight, the tradition of the Yule Log lives on in a few more modern ways.

1600s: Yule Log as Tasty Treat: The Bûche de Noël

One of the earliest ways the Yule Log tradition evolved from the early rituals is actually quite a tasty one. In the 1600s—when people started burning more reasonably sized logs in their fireplaces—bakers started paying homage to Yule Log traditions with a sponge cake-and-meringue creation now most commonly known as the Bûche de Noël (French for "Yule Log"). The first known recipe for this log-shaped treat appeared in Gervaise Markham's 1615 *The English Huswife*. Thanks to Gervaise and other bakers of the time, there was now another, easier way to celebrate the Yule—and it didn't hurt that the treat was tasty as heck and looked cool, too (like a giant, more interesting and woodsy Swiss Roll). In the 19th century, Parisian bakers did as Parisian bakers do, improving upon the recipe and popularizing it. Today, the unique creation is seen in many bakeries and on many tables each Christmas season. Turn to page 37 to try your hand at baking a Bûche de Noël this year!

1960s: The Yule Hits the Tube

You may be surprised to learn that long before you could find hundreds of Yule Log videos at your fingertips on YouTube (more on that later), a Yule Log video could be seen playing on television screens across America. In 1966, a big exec at New York television station WPIX had a great idea for how he could give his workers some time off around the holidays—and to bring a little free holiday cheer to homes across

the city. He conceived of *The Yule Log*, a 17-second-long video (with music!) that would play on loop during some late-night and early-morning hours on Christmas Eve and Christmas. This gave newscasters some time off, and allowed those who didn't have a fireplace to enjoy the cozy atmosphere that a Yule Log can cast on a blustery holiday evening. Win-winter-win! It was a huge hit, and went on to be rebroadcast for 23 consecutive years. (In 1970, the video was re-shot to play for a much-improved seven minutes, which gave it a more seamless and interesting look.) The program was canceled in 1990, but it found new life online in the late '90s.

The Yule Log undoubtedly served as inspiration for the many VHS and DVD versions that cropped up and allowed people to burn a virtual log during their Christmas parties, as well as the myriad videos now available to stream online (you can check out the original at TheYuleLog.com. As that site states, the original video "has

often been imitated, but never duplicated").

Today: Yule Log starts cropping up on YouTube and TVs everywhere

Fast-forward to today, where there are nearly 100,000 yule log videos available for streaming on YouTube alone. The versions range from the classic (crackling fire sounds, Christmas sounds, and the like) to videos that include animals, animated characters, digital snow, and more. There are even some featuring celebrities and pop-culture characters—internet cat sensation Lil BUB; Darth Vader; Michael Bublé; Ron Swanson; Disney characters like Woody and Mickey; Doctor Who; and even the star of the season himself: Jesus! Whether you're a Yule Log purist or prefer a more quirky variety, there is a Yule Log video out there for you, and you can play it on loop for hours and hours year after year. (No one tell the pagans how easy we have it.)

The most-played YouTube Yule Log video, from "Christmas Time," has more than **14 million views.**

Inventive Uses for Your Itty-Bitty Yule Log

Even if you don't have time to go chop down an oak tree and burn it for twelve days, you can reap some of the benefits of the Yule Log tradition this holiday season now that you have the *Mini Yule Log*. Here are a few ideas on where to showcase yours!

- Put it on your desktop to ward off office evils (paper cuts, computer viruses, Doris).

- Place it on your nightstand to inspire dreams of sugar plum fairies.

- Create a tiny Christmas scene on top of your fireplace—cut stockings out of felt and affix them to your itty bitty hearth. Mantle meta!

- Bring it with you to meetings to give your office manager a hint to turn up the heat.

- Gaze into the flames to see your future. (Spoiler alert: You won't see anything, but it will be a welcome distraction from your holiday stress.)

A Yule by Any Other Name

In English alone, there are at least a dozen variations on the name for this mysterious log thought to fend off evil spirits. Here are just a few of the many strange names that exist for it:

- Gule Block
- Stock of the Mock
- Yule Clog
- Christmas Block
- Festival Block
- The Christmas Old Wife

Bûche de Noël
Recipe

Pay a tasty homage to the Yule Log with this showstopper, sure to delight at your next family feast. You'll need some buttercream frosting—vanilla or chocolate, your choice—already made. Traditionally, the cake is also topped with small meringue mushrooms—add those if you are feeling fun(gus)!

INGREDIENTS

2 cups heavy cream
½ cup and ¼ cup confectioners'
   sugar, divided
½ cup and ⅓ cup unsweetened cocoa
   powder, divided
1 teaspoon and 1½ teaspoons vanilla
   extract, divided
6 eggs, separated
½ cup white sugar
⅛ teaspoon salt
¾–1 cup vanilla or chocolate
   buttercream icing for filling

DIRECTIONS

1. Line a 10" x 15" pan with parchment paper and preheat your oven to 375 degrees.

2. In a large bowl, whip together the heavy cream, ½ cup of the confectioners' sugar, ½ cup of the cocoa, and 1 teaspoon of the vanilla extract until thick and stiff. Refrigerate.

3. In an electric mixer, mix the egg yolks and ½ cup of the white sugar until thick and well incorporated. Add in the remaining ⅓ cup of cocoa powder, remaining vanilla, and the salt. Then, in a separate bowl and with clean beater, whip the egg whites until they form soft peaks. Gradually add the remaining white sugar and beat until the mixture forms stiff peaks. Gently fold into the yolk mix you made and refrigerated earlier. Pour the batter into the prepared pan.

4. Bake for 12 to 15 minutes. Meanwhile, sift the rest of the confectioners' sugar onto a clean dish towel. When cake is finished cooking, loosen the sides and turn the cake onto the sugared towel. Remove and discard the parchment paper. Starting at the short side of the cake, roll the cake up with the towel and let it cool for 30 minutes.

5. Unroll the cake, remove from the towel, and spread with chocolate or vanilla buttercream, stopping 1 inch from the edge of the cake. Again starting at the short end, roll the cake and filling into a large swirl. Place the seam side down on a serving platter, cover, and refrigerate until you're ready to serve.

You can also add icing to the exterior and drag a fork down the length of the log, adding some bark-like detail to make this feel even more like the trees ancient folks burned to bring their villages good luck!

This book has been bound using handcraft methods
and Smyth-sewn to ensure durability.

The cover and interior were designed by
Joshua McDonnell.

The text was written by
Conor Riordan.